W9-DEY-467
Cuba

Discovering Cultures

Cuba

Sharon Gordon

Benchmark Books
MARSHALL CAVENDISH
NEW YORK

With thanks to Uva de Aragón, Associate Director, Cuban Research Institute, Florida International University, for the careful review of this manuscript.

Benchmark Books
Marshall Cavendish
99 White Plains Road
Tarrytown, New York 10591-9001
www.marshallcavendish.com

Library of Congress Cataloging-in-Publication Data

Gordon, Sharon.
Cuba / by Sharon Gordon.
p. cm. — (Discovering cultures)
Summary: Highlights the geography, people, food, schools, recreation, celebrations, and language of Cuba.
Includes bibliographical references and index.
ISBN 0-7614-1517-3
1. Cuba—Juvenile literature. [1. Cuba.] I. Title. II. Series.
F1758.5 .G67 2003
972.91—dc21 2002015302

Photo Research by Candlepants Incorporated

Cover Photo: David Foreman/Eye Ubiquitous/Corbis

The photographs in this book are used by permission and through the courtesy of; *Lucid Images/Mark Downey*: 1, 4-5, 8-9,10, 14, 27 (top & bottom), 37, back cover. *Corbis*: Bob Krist, 6, 12, 18; James Davis:Eye Ubiquitous, 11; Earl & Nazima Kowall, 15; Jan Butchofsky-Houser, 16-17; Paul Seheult: Eye Ubiquitous, 19; Richard Bickel, 20-21, 23, Amos Nachoum, 21 (right), 36; Jeremy Horner, 22 ,24; David H.Wells, 26; Bill Gentile, 28; Christopher J. Morris, 30, 33; Ed Quinn, 31; Francoise de Mulder, 32; Pablo Corral Vega, 34; Reuters NewMedia Inc., 38-39, 44 (right); AFP, 40, 44 (left); Bettmann, 55.

Map and illustrations by Salvatore Murdocca
Book design by Virginia Pope

Cover: *Statue of José Martí*; Title page: *Smiling Cuban girl*

Printed in Hong Kong
1 3 5 6 4 2

Turn the Pages...

¡Hola! (Hello!)

Welcome to the sunny island of Cuba. Step ashore and discover our land and culture.

Schoolchildren smile from an open window.

Where in the World Is Cuba?

The island of Cuba is located south of the United States. In fact, it is only 90 miles (145 kilometers) from Key West, Florida. Cuba is surrounded by three major bodies of water: the Caribbean Sea to the south, the Atlantic Ocean to the northeast, and the Gulf of Mexico to the northwest. It is the largest island in the West Indies, a group of islands that stretches between North and South America.

One of Cuba's many beautiful beaches

The Republic of Cuba is made up of one main island and more than 1,600 tiny islands and *cayos* (sand reefs). The main island is nearly 750 miles (1,207 kilometers) long, which is about the distance from New York to Chicago. It ranges from only 25 miles (40 kilometers) wide in the west to 120 miles (193 kilometers) wide in the east. Cuba is almost the size of

Gulf of Mexico
Havana
Atlantic Ocean
Caribbean Sea
Pico Turquino
N
NW
NE
W
E
SW
SE
S

the state of Pennsylvania. Its fine beaches and coral reefs stretch for more than 2,000 miles (almost 4,000 kilometers).

The land of Cuba is mostly rolling plains and river basins. Along the southeast coast are the rugged Sierra Maestra. These high mountains include Pico Turquino. At 6,560 feet (2,000 meters), Pico Turquino is the highest point in Cuba.

Cuba has a semi-tropical climate, with an average temperature of 77 degrees Fahrenheit (24 degrees Celsius). Gentle trade winds blow from west to east off the ocean and help keep the temperature from getting too hot. Cuba's dry season runs from November to April. The rainy season lasts from May to October. During these summer months, it rains almost every day. But after a short rain shower, the clear blue skies return.

During the rainy season, hurricanes hit the country. Hurricanes are strong tropical storms that have high winds and

Western Cuba's lush landscape

A tobacco farmer gathers leaves.

soaking rains. Cuba has an average of one hurricane every other year. A strong hurricane can cause serious damage to the island, its people, and its crops.

Cuba's rich soil and warm climate make it perfect for farming. Cuba's main crop is sugarcane. Most sugarcane is made into table sugar, but some is used to make molasses or rum. Cuban sugar is shipped around the globe, ending up in all kinds of sweet treats. Cubans love sugary snacks, with ice cream being at the top of their list.

Cuba's most famous crop is tobacco, which is made into cigars. Cuban cigars are considered the best in the world. Cuban farmers also grow coffee beans, rice, potatoes, oranges, and mangoes.

The Capitol Building in Old Havana

The capital of Cuba is Havana, its largest city. Havana was founded by Spanish settlers in 1515. It is an amazing blend of the old and the new. In Old Havana, you can find narrow streets and historic buildings that were built as early as the 1500s. Many buildings are painted in pastel colors. The rest of Havana is more modern, with wide streets and high-rise buildings. Havana's Plaza de la Revolución (Plaza of the Revolution) is the center of the Cuban government. The National Library, National Theater, and many other buildings are located in the Plaza.

Havana and its harbor

Sierra de los Órganos
(Mountains of the organs)

The Sierra de los Órganos is a mountain range in the western part of Cuba. The range was given its name by Spanish settlers who thought the rows of rolling mountains looked like the pipes of an organ. In the Sierra de los Órganos, you will find *mogotes*, some of the most unusual mountains in the world. These steep, flattopped limestone mountains rise up out of the land. They are covered with thick green foliage. Some *mogotes* have caves and tunnels inside that were formed by underground rivers. These caves are amazing to visit, but watch out for the bats!

What Makes Cuba Cuban?

Cubans speak Spanish, the national language.

The people of Cuba are as warm and inviting as the climate. Most Cubans tend to be open and generous to each other and to strangers. A Cuban neighborhood is relaxed and friendly. It is a place to put up your feet, sip a cool drink, and chat with family and friends. The Cuban lifestyle is reflected in the casual dress. Except for special occasions, most Cubans wear cool, loose clothing in the warm climate.

Cuba is a true "melting pot" of races. The original Cubans were people called Taínos and Ciboneyes. But there are very few native people living in Cuba today. After Columbus claimed the land for Spain, Spanish settlers came to the island. Today, many Cubans are the descendants of the

The Cathedral of Havana

Spanish settlers. Others are the descendants of black slaves who were brought to Cuba from Africa in the sixteenth century. About one-third of modern Cubans are a mix of Spanish and African heritage. Chinese workers came to Cuba in the mid-1800s. Many of their families still live there today. Even though Cubans may come from different backgrounds, they speak Spanish, Cuba's national language.

The blending of cultures in Cuba can be seen easily in everything from religion to music. The Spanish settlers brought their Roman Catholic religion to the island. One of Cuba's most popular religions is Santería. It mixes Roman Catholicism with the religion of the Yoruba people who were brought from Africa as slaves.

Both Catholic saints and *orishas* (Yoruban gods) are cherished by the Cuban people.

Music is at the heart of Cuban culture. Whenever there is a celebration or a party, there is always music and dancing. The Spanish settlers brought classical and folk music to the island. African music was rhythmic and bold. Many Cuban bands use both African drums and the Spanish guitar to create their own popular songs. Cuban jazz also blends African and Cuban rhythms. Once a year, the International Jazz Festival is held in Havana. Artists and fans from around the world come to play, listen, and dance.

Cubans are known for their love of dancing. Most Cuban dance music, such as the rumba, the cha-cha, and the mambo, has its roots in Africa. Today's popular salsa music started among Cuban musicians in New York City in the 1960s. Salsa is played in Cuban restau-

Drums give Cuban music a bold sound.

rants and clubs and at parties, along with the more modern rhythm called *timba*.

Cubans have always enjoyed art. Cuba's art reflects the bright colors found in nature all around the island. In the past, the island was a convenient stop for artists and writers traveling between North and South America. By the beginning of the 1800s, Havana was considered an important cultural city. Books and newspapers began to be published. The Cuban love of poetry was born. In the 1800s, many famous poets began to write about their dream of freedom from Spain. Some were forced to leave the country because of their writing. Far from Cuba, they wrote moving poems about how much they missed their beautiful homeland. One such poet was José Martí. His poetry is still read and memorized by Cubans today.

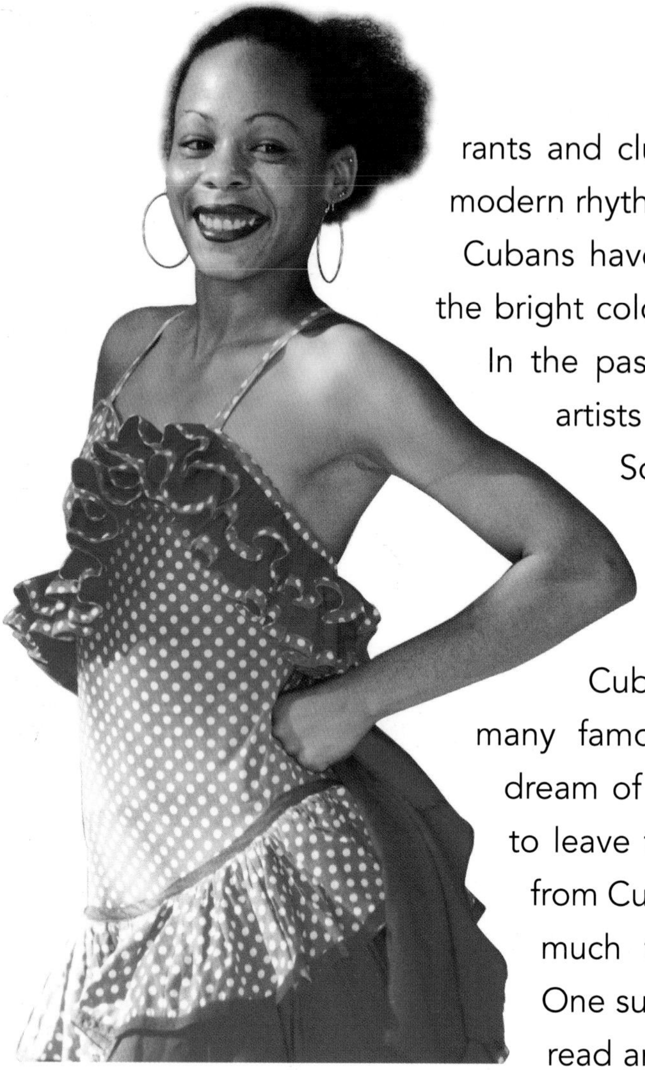

A Cuban folk dancer

Many Cubans came to the United States when Fidel Castro took over the country in 1959. These immigrants brought their culture with them when they settled in south Florida. Cuban cooking, music, and traditions are kept alive by these Cuban-American families. Today, there are more than one million people of Cuban origin living in the United States. So many Cubans live in Miami, Florida, that one neighborhood there is called "Little Havana."

Palmas reales
(Royal palms)

When Christopher Columbus first landed on the island of Cuba in 1492, he said it was "the most beautiful land" he had ever seen. With its *palmas reales* and miles of sunny beaches, any modern visitor would agree. In the rural areas, the *palmas reales* have always been very important. Their stems are woven into houses and their dried leaves are used for the roofs. The fruit of the palm is fed to hogs, and its oil is used in cooking. Almost every part of the tree is used for something. It is no wonder that the *palma real* is a protected tree.

Living in Cuba

After Fidel Castro took over the government, Cuba became a communist country. In a communist country, the government owns everything. People cannot own their own homes or businesses. For many years, Cuba received help from another communist country, the Soviet Union. But when the Soviet Union collapsed in 1991, Cuba lost its support. The Soviets stopped buying Cuban goods and products. They stopped sending Cuba low-cost oil. Since then, Cubans have been living in difficult days with limited amounts of food, fuel, and medical supplies.

Conditions began to improve slightly in the early 2000s. New laws have

A farming family

Fishing boats in Havana

allowed some people to open and own their own businesses. Many women now work outside of the home and there is free child care. Cubans who live in the cities may work in factories and restaurants. Those who live in rural areas may work on farms that grow sugarcane, coffee, fruits, and vegetables. Some farmers raise cattle. There are fishing jobs in the seaports, and some mining jobs in the western mountains.

Most Cubans live in the cities. About two million people live in Havana alone. But Cubans do not own their

This old car still gets around.

own homes or apartments. They live in apartments owned by the state, and they pay rent to the Cuban government. Many buildings are in need of repairs. And since cars and gasoline are very expensive, many city dwellers use bicycles to get around. Others take a bus or walk. Farmers in the suburbs also use bicycles for transportation when fuel is not available.

Traditional Cuban food is colorful and delicious. It includes many tropical fruits, such as *plátanos* (plantains) and pineapples. Cuban food blends Spanish and African tastes. It is spicy but not hot. Most meals contain yams, rice, beans and other locally grown food. Dishes with a Spanish flair are made with olive oil, sizzling onions, green bell peppers, and lots of garlic. Slowly simmered beans and stews are popular. So are dishes like *arroz con pollo* (rice with chicken). Delicious shellfish from local waters are enjoyed with a lot of garlic.

Food is rationed, which means Cubans are allowed only a small amount of basic foods. Sometimes they must wait in line to purchase their items. It is difficult to make many traditional dishes when meat, milk, oil, and spices are hard to get. But Cuban cooks are creative. They have learned to turn simple ingredients into a flavorful meal.

Cubans wait in line for food.

The National Hotel in Havana

Each year, more and more visitors come to visit Cuba's beautiful beaches and resorts. Hotels that were once owned by the government are now run by international companies. These companies make sure the hotels are up-to-date. New construction jobs are being created. As new buildings go up and old ones are repaired, more workers are needed to work in local restaurants and hotels. These new opportunities are giving Cubans the hope that the difficult days will soon be over.

Let's Eat!

Moros y Cristianos
(Moors and Christians)

Moros y Cristianos can be made many different ways, depending on the kinds of beans and spices available. It is considered one of Cuba's national dishes. It contains the common Cuban ingredients of rice, peppers, garlic, and onions. Ask an adult to help you prepare this recipe.

Ingredients:

2 tablespoons olive oil

1 chopped onion

1 clove minced garlic

1 sliced green pepper

2 chopped tomatoes

8 ounces cooked black beans

6 ounces rice

3/4 pint cold water

salt and pepper to taste

Wash your hands. Heat the oil in a saucepan and add the onion, garlic, and pepper. Saute until tender. Mix in tomatoes and stir until it thickens. Season to taste and add the beans. Then add the rice and water. Cover and simmer until the water is absorbed. Can be served with *plátanos*.

School Days

Everyone goes to public school in Cuba, since there are no private schools. All children must go to primary school between the ages of six and twelve to study math, reading, and history. The school year runs from September to June and has about forty weeks of school per year. Most students wear uniforms. Education is free from preschool to college. The government provides students with books and other materials.

Cuba has a high literacy rate, which means that most people can read and write. Although Spanish is the native language, students also learn other languages. In the past, English was considered an important language for Cuban students to learn. But when Cuba became a communist country, many children studied Russian. Today, learning English has a practical, new importance. Cuban workers must be able to communicate with the growing number of English-speaking tourists.

A student wears his school uniform.

Cuban children work hard in school.

After completing primary school, students attend secondary school. There they study languages, technology, history, math, chemistry, and biology. Many city children go to boarding schools in the country. They live in the school and work in the fields. Many go home on weekends or for vacations.

Students who do well in secondary school may attend college. There are several universities to choose from in Cuba, including the University of Havana, which

Schoolgirls take a break.

High school students work in a field.

is the largest. In college, they might study to become a teacher or engineer. When they graduate, the government tells them where they will work. This is how students repay their country for the free education.

Cuba has special schools for some of its students. For talented athletes there are sports schools like the Sports Institute. There, they can train in their sport while taking regular academic classes. The National School of Art and the National School of Ballet are for students who are good at music, dance, and art. Children with disabilities are given one-to-one attention in other schools.

Cuban schools stress the importance of both education and service. All Cuban children must do some kind of physical work in addition to their regular classroom studies. They might help plant a garden or work on a farm. Other students might clean up part of the town or sweep the sidewalks. Older students might learn a trade. They are taught important on-the-job skills. They learn about their responsibility to society.

La Guantanamera
(Woman from Guantánamo)

The popular Cuban song, "La Guantanamera," is based on a poem written by José Martí and published in 1891 in the book *Versos Sencillos* (Simple Verses). The chorus and music to the song were added years later and it became a popular hit around the world.

Just for Fun

Playing baseball at the Capitol

Cuban people are fun-loving by nature. Sports are enjoyed by young and old. Baseball is the most popular sport in Cuba. It was brought to Cuba from the United States around 1865. Young children play baseball at home and at school. In Cuba, an empty lot or field can quickly turn into a baseball diamond.

Baseball is not a high-paying sport in Cuba. All sports are controlled and supported by the government. But this has not stopped the Cuban people from playing and loving baseball. The Cuban baseball team won the gold medal at the 1992 and the 1996 Olympic Games. Their players are admired around the world. Cuba's all-star team even played in Baltimore, Maryland, in 1999. Some Cuban players, such as Orlando "El Duque" Hernández and his brother Liván, left their homeland to play professional baseball in the United States.

Boxing is also very popular in Cuba. Children are introduced to the sport in school, and if they are talented and interested, they can receive training. It is a sport that requires excellent physical health and strong muscles and quick feet. Cuba has produced some outstanding boxers over the years, some of whom have won Olympic gold medals.

Tourists who come to Cuba enjoy its many fine beaches. Cuba has a jagged coastline, and so it has many different kinds of beaches. El Caney is an unusual beach with reddish-brown pebbles instead of sand. Varadero is Cuba's most famous and popular beach. This 10-mile (16-kilometer) stretch on the north coast has fine, white sand that is very smooth to walk on.

A Cuban boy practices his boxing moves.

Relaxing after school on the Malecón

Varadero has many beautiful hotels. Here the sea is shallow, and vacationers can walk far out into the clear, blue water.

The Malecón is a long seawall that runs along the Havana harbor. It is a popular place to fish, hang out, and enjoy the beautiful sea. Children often gather

A somersault off the Malecón

there after school. On summer nights, Cubans stroll down the sidewalk and enjoy the ocean breeze.

Relaxing with neighbors in Cuba is not hard to do. Since the weather is warm year-round, Cuban families might leave their doors open on weekends for family and friends to visit. Neighbors might watch television together or gather at a local

Dancing in the park

park to discuss news and share stories. Since Cubans are not able to travel very much, they are very curious about other places and cultures around the world. They often will ask questions of visiting travelers to learn more about their countries.

Dominoes

Next to baseball, the second-favorite Cuban pastime is dominoes. The good thing about dominoes is that it can be played by anyone, not just those in good shape. Two to four people of any age can play at any time of year. It is a favorite way to relax. Senior citizens especially like to play dominoes with friends in parks or recreation areas.

Let's Celebrate!

Most Cuban holidays are political. They celebrate the birthdays of important leaders or war victories. The biggest celebration is July 26, called the Remembrance of the National Rebellion. This national holiday celebrates the day when Fidel Castro and his revolutionaries attacked an army post in the city of

Students remember José Martí's birthday.

Santiago in 1953. Although they were defeated, it was the beginning of Castro's successful struggle to take over the government. The day is celebrated with lively festivities. People dress in costumes, attend street parties and parades, and listen to speeches by the politicians.

The Remembrance happens at the same time as an old tradition known as Carnaval. Cubans celebrate Carnaval from late July to early August. It began as a celebration of the end of the sugarcane harvest. When the harvest was over, Cubans could enjoy a time of rest and relaxation. Although Castro ended the celebration of Carnaval from 1991 through 1996, it was

Ready for the parade

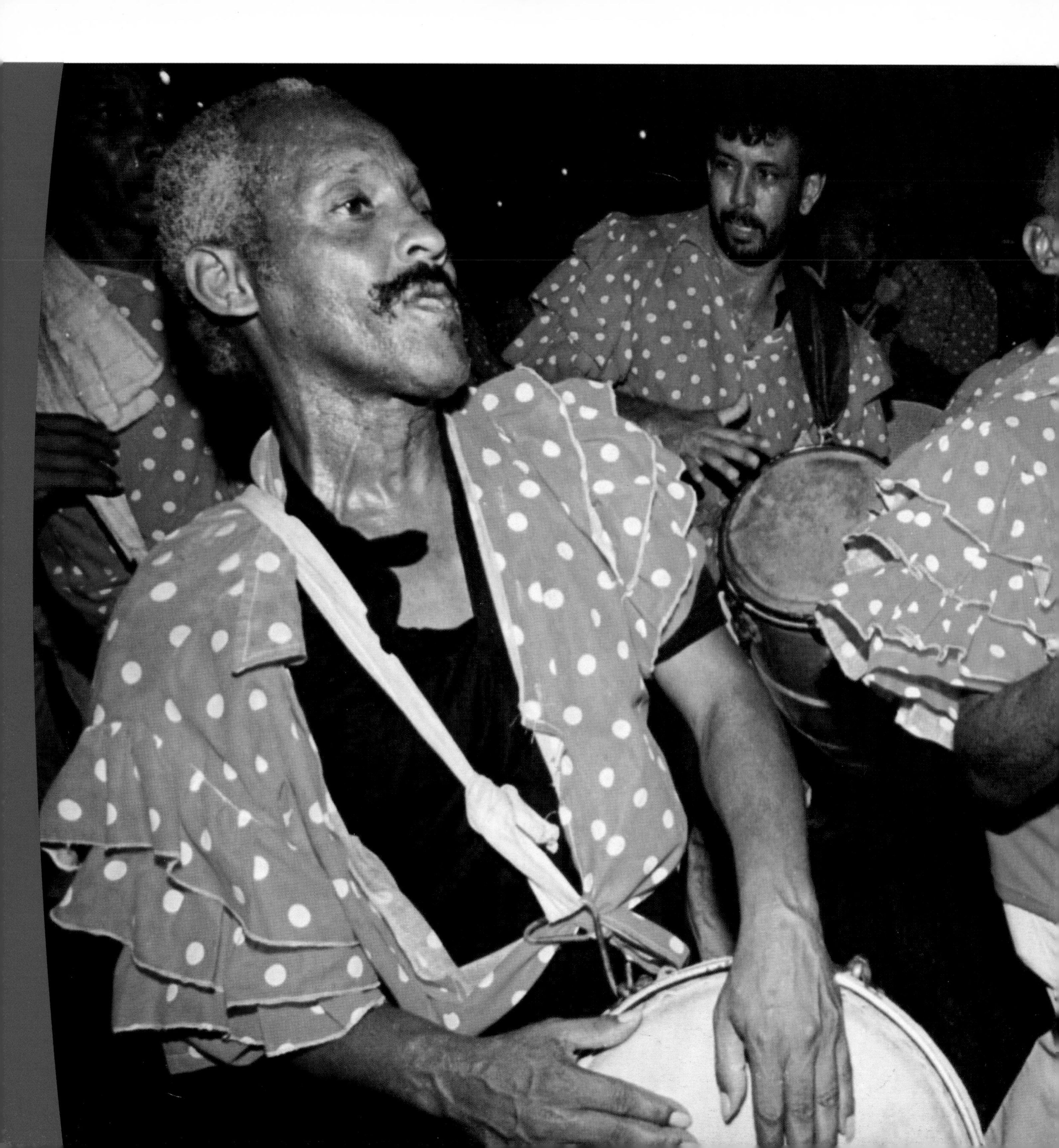

revived in 1997 when conditions began to improve.

Carnaval is a lot like the Mardi Gras celebration each year in New Orleans. It is the biggest celebration of the year with weeks of parades and street parties. Women dress in festive clothes and dancers wearing colorful costumes perform in the streets. Carnaval lets Cubans celebrate their heritage through food, music, and dancing.

For many years, the celebration of Christmas on December 25 had been canceled because the government said it interfered with the sugarcane harvest. But in December of 1998, Cuba's daily newspaper reported that Christmas was once again an official holiday. This was welcomed by the Cuban people. They could decorate their homes with lights and candles. They were allowed to display

Drummers at Carnaval

Christmas trees. Even government stores were selling plastic trees and decorations. Cubans enjoy having another day to rest and spend with their families.

Time to decorate the Christmas tree

Comparsas

During carnivals, dancing groups known as *comparsas* often perform in the streets. They wear the colorful costumes that were popular during the days when the Spanish controlled the island. In years past, each neighborhood would form its own *comparsa* and members would practice their routine. They would compete against other *comparsas* in a large parade. Today, the competition between the dancing groups has stopped. But the elaborate costumes and lively dancing of the *comparsas* are still a wonderful tradition that can be seen during Cuban street festivals and celebrations.

The Cuban flag has two white stripes and three blue ones. Blue stands for the ocean that surrounds the island. White stands for the pure ideas of the Cuban leaders. The red in the triangle on the left side of the flag stands for the blood of the people who died for Cuba. The white star in the center of the triangle stands for the independence of the Cuban people.

There are two kinds of money in Cuba: the Cuban peso and the U.S. dollar. The exchange rate changes often, but in 2002 2.34 pesos equaled one U.S. dollar.

Count in Spanish

English	Spanish	Say it like this:
one	uno	OO-noh
two	dos	DOHS
three	tres	TRACE
four	cuatro	KWAH-troh
five	cinco	THEEN-koh
six	seis	SAYSS
seven	siete	see-EH-tay
eight	ocho	OH-choh
nine	nueve	NWEH-veh
ten	diez	DEE-ehth

Glossary

Carnaval Cuba's biggest holiday, celebrated with parades and street fairs.

comparsas (com-PAR-sahs) Dancing groups that perform at Cuban festivals.

foliage Cluster of leaves, flowers, and branches.

Malecón (mah-leh-CONE) Seawall that protects a portion of Havana.

orishas (oh-REE-shahs) Yoruban gods of the Santería religion.

plátanos (PLAH-tah-nohs) Green starchy fruit shaped like a banana.

rumba (ROOM-bah) Lively Cuban ballroom dance and music.

Santería (San-ta-REE-ya) Religion that worships Catholic saints and African gods.

salsa (SAHL-sah) Popular dance music started by Cuban musicians in New York City.

sofrito (so-FREE-toe) Cuban sauce of onions, green peppers, and garlic.

Proud to Be Cuban

Alicia Alonso (1921–)

Alicia Alonso was born in Havana and is considered one of the world's best ballerinas. She began dancing as a child and started taking dance lessons in Havana in 1931. Alonso traveled to New York City and studied at the School of American Ballet. She gained an international reputation for her excellent skills and style. She returned to Havana and founded the Ballet Alicia Alonso in 1948. It was renamed the National Ballet of Cuba in 1959. Today, the National Ballet of Cuba is known all over the world for its outstanding performers.

Orlando "El Duque (The Duke)" Hernández (1965–)

Orlando Hernández left Cuba in 1997. He began his American career with the New York Yankees in the minor leagues, but was called up to the majors to replace an injured pitcher. Hernández won his first big-league game against Tampa Bay and finished the year with a 12–4 record. In the postseason games, Hernández had key wins in the play-offs and the World Series. El Duque quickly became an important part of the pitching staff. In 2000, he became the first foreign-born pitcher to start a season opener for the club. In the play-offs of that year, Hernández became the first pitcher to win his first eight postseason games. The Duke of Havana quickly became the pride of New York.

José Martí (1853–1895)

José Martí is Cuba's best-loved patriot. He dreamed of an independent Cuba, free from Spain. Because of his views, he was sent to jail. Then he was thrown out of the country and moved to Spain. There, he earned a law degree and began to write essays encouraging a Cuban revolution. He eventually settled in the United States where he worked to gain support for his cause. In 1895, Martí and his forces landed in Cuba to join the fight for independence. In a few years, Spain lost control of most of the country, except for the coastal towns. Thousand of Cubans died in that long rebellion, including José Martí at the age of 42. But Cuba finally gained its freedom. To this day, Cubans remember this brave hero and celebrate his life. The beautiful song *La Guantanamera* has made his verses famous around the world, and many statues have been built in his honor. Cuban children even memorize his poetry in school. José Martí's birthday, January 28, is celebrated as a holiday in Cuba.

Find Out More

Books

Countries of the World: Cuba by Mark Cramer. Gareth Stevens Publishing, Wisconsin, 2000.

Cuba: After the Revolution by Bernard Wolf. Dutton Children's Books, New York, 1999.

A True Book: Cuba by Christine Petersen and David Petersen. Children's Press, New York, 2001.

Faces and Places: Cuba by Kathryn Stevens. The Child's World, Minnesota, 2002.

Children of Cuba by Frank Staub. Carolrhoda Books, Minnesota, 1996.

Web sites

http://www.yahooligans.com/around_the_world/countries/cuba/

Links to photographs and maps of Cuba, plus numerous sites on the country's culture and history.

http://sunsite.berkeley.edu/KidsClick!

Type in *Cuba* and this Web search will list sites on travel, architecture, history, and geography.

Video

Cuba: Island of Dreams. International Video Network Entertainment, 1996. 52 min.

Index

Page numbers for illustrations are in **boldface.**

About the Author

Sharon Gordon has written many nature and science books for young children. She has worked as an advertising copywriter and a book club editor. She is writing other books for the *Discovering Cultures* series. Sharon and her husband Bruce have three teenage children, Douglas, Katie, and Laura, and one spoiled pooch, Samantha. They live in Midland Park, New Jersey. The family especially enjoys traveling to the Outer Banks of North Carolina. After she puts her three children through college, Sharon hopes to visit the many exciting places she has come to love through her writing and research.